He Who Laughs

Lasts and Lasts and Lasts . . .

He Who Laughs

Lasts and Lasts and Lasts . . .

by
Roy H. Hicks, D.D.

HARRISON HOUSE
Tulsa, Oklahoma

Unless otherwise indicated,
all Scripture quotations are taken from
the *King James Version* of the Bible.

12th Printing
Over 65,000 in Print

He Who Laughs Lasts and Lasts and Lasts . . .
ISBN 0-89274-003-5
Copyright © 1976 by Roy H. Hicks, D.D.
P. O. Box 4113
San Marcos, California 92069

Published by Harrison House, Inc.
P. O. Box 35035
Tulsa, Oklahoma 74153

Contents

ABOUT THE AUTHOR

This is a book on laughter, and includes humor, but I'm not joking when I say, I want to introduce you to a perfect man.

I suppose some would think it unwise, if not dangerous, to introduce a man as "perfect." But I'm going to. I want to present to those readers who are as yet unfamiliar with his writings and his ministry, Dr. Roy Hicks.

David said, "Mark the perfect man, and behold the upright, for the end of that man is peace" (Psalm 37:37). Simple study will define the Biblical use of the word "perfect": mature, complete, full-grown, fruitful. It is not an ascription of fastidious flawlessness, but of godly growingness.

And in telling us it is right to "mark" a perfect man—to identfy him before onlookers—it also tells us how we will know the man is perfect: "the end—the manifest developments over long observation—the end of that man is peace."

I've known Roy Hicks for over 15 years. I've walked in a close enough association that I can say with candor and conviction: the fruit of this man's life is peace. His pastoral work bore that fruit, his role as a pastor to pastors has demonstrated it, his teaching ministry to thousands in conferences around the world shows it, and in the greatest test of all—his home and family—the "end of that man is peace."

Please meet my friend. He's a trustworthy teacher. Someone you can learn with . . . and be free to laugh with.

> Pastor Jack Hayford
>
> "The Church On The Way"
>
> Van Nuys, California

ABOUT THE BOOK

Roy Hicks always gives me something to chew on. I like that. I like for a teacher or a preacher to give me some good spiritual food from the Word of God which leaves me with something to chew on . . . something to digest . . . some meat. Roy Hicks does that. He gets me to looking at spiritual truths and seeing them from a different perspective.

I guarantee you Chapter IX will give you a new perspective on some things. Did you ever wonder about God's foreknowledge? Timelessness? Predestination? Man's free will? Just flip over there and read that chapter first to whet your appetite. It won't spoil the order of the book for you.

"Laughter is joy flowing . . .", Hicks writes. "Laughter is more of an attitude than an audible, physical expression." You'll learn a lot from his book about the great source of joy available to the church—but long overlooked. You'll learn how to laugh at the devil. How to laugh through circumstances to victory . . . to liberty . . . to health and strength. How to live (not die) laughing.

Kenneth Hagin

INTRODUCTION

The godless philosopher Nietzsche once said, "The Christians would have to look more saved if they hoped to persuade him." Nietzsche's comment was no doubt valid. Even casual observation today would witness to the truth of his statement. Many Christians have never entered into the joy of their Lord. If they have, they failed to notify their faces. Josh Billings said, "Laffing is the sensation of pheeling good all over and showing it principally in one spot." That spot should radiate the joy of the Lord.

Matthew Henry said, "Holy joy will be oil to the wheels of obedience." Someone else said, "Laughter is the spirit's white plumed helmet." When you put sound to joy it will come out as laughter, just as sorrow will manifest itself in crying. Blessed are the people who know the joyful sound.

Our greatest incentive to be joyful and happy is found in Proverbs 17:22a:

"A merry heart doeth good like a medicine." A young child trying to recall this verse said, "A merry heart doeth good like a baby aspirin." One wonders whether we really believe the Scriptures. Will a merry heart take the place of a medicine? Even if it helps us a little . . . we should laugh a lot!

A merry heart is not a natural heart . . . it takes conscious effort to keep it merry. Joy is one of the fruits of the Spirit which needs to be cultivated. Jesus had much to say about joy and the fullness of joy.

May this book serve to remind you that believers can rejoice . . . in fact we, as believers, are commanded to do so in Philippians 4:4, "Rejoice in the Lord always: and again I say, rejoice." Joy is tied into faith in Philippians 1:25 and to hope in Romans 15:13.

Being happy, glad, and joyful is a good thermometer of one's faith in God. Kenneth Hagin, a great man of faith, has so many wonderful experiences that prove this to be correct.

Paul Rader is quoted as saying, "When God chooses a man He puts laughter into his life." One of Jack Hayford's recent choruses, entitled "Lord you cause my heart to laugh and make my mouth to sing," is indicative of the spirit of the great charismatic revival of this day . . . a revival of joy and happiness! May this book and this subject encourage your relationship with our Lord Jesus in such a fashion that your joy would become full, resulting in laughter that will cause you to last . . . and last . . . and last!

Chapter I

LAUGHTER, AN ATTITUDE

The subject of laughter arouses many responses. Some will say, "I don't think it is right just to laugh everything away." This response is born of a fear that harasses some people who feel they must experience a sense of anxiety or worry or they would feel they were being frivolous or too light-hearted. I heard someone remark, "I think people who laugh a lot are just giddy." This impression may be a correct one about some people, but it does not justify the counsel of those who would instruct us to go about our daily tasks continually with a sober countenance. Someone else said, "But their laugh is so hollow sounding it irritates me!" A statement like that is altogether true about much of the laughter that assaults our ears . . . some tinny, some raucous, some irksome . . . but this does not justify our determined ignorance and neglect of a great truth.

Laughter should be considered more of an attitude than an audible, physical expression. Webster's dictionary says that attitude is a "bodily posture showing a mental state, emotion, or mood." Speaking from the spiritual viewpoint it must be an attitude first, physical second. Attitudes are formed by conviction . . . conviction is not formed by attitude. Christians who have developed strong convictions as to who they are, where they are going, who God is, His love, His Word, His Son, have healthier attitudes toward life than those who do not have such deep-seated convictions. The attitude of the majority of the unconverted is, "What is to be will be . . . you just have to take the bad with the good . . . that's the way the cookie crumbles . . . or, that's the way the ball bounces." While this may seem to be a better attitude than the one that says that life is full of nothing but toil and trouble, it still lacks depth and conviction. It is an attitude that is not able to say:

> "And we know that all things work together for good to them that love God, to them that are the called according to His purpose." Romans 8:28.

> "If God be for us, who can be against us?" Romans 8:31b.

Laughter is joy flowing, happiness showing, countenance glowing. An attitude of self pity, "Who's to blame?" "Pin-point the fault," is never expressed in joy. An attitude of trust, faith, hope, and love will find expression in delight. Parents who frequently lie to their children will eat the bitter fruit of seeing their children distrust and lose faith in them. When promises are made to children—promises repeatedly broken—they will eventually hear the child's response of, "they probably won't go," "it will never happen," "oh, never mind, you won't do it anyway." A child reared in this atmosphere of broken pledges is not a happy, secure one and usually feels threatened by the future. Many adults continue to have a flow of joy into adulthood because their attitudes are healthy, brought over from a positive attitude as a child.

Somehow we seem to catch the attitude of our Lord Jesus toward being joyful and happy. In John 15:11 Jesus said:

> "These things have I spoken unto you, that my joy might remain in you, and that your joy might be full."

In John 16:22 Jesus said:

"And ye now therefore have sorrow: but I will see you again, and your heart shall rejoice, and your joy no man taketh from you."

Verse 24 says:

"Hitherto have ye asked nothing in my name; ask and ye shall receive, that your joy may be full."

Phillip states ". . . that your joy may be overflowing." No one reading these Scriptures can for a moment doubt Christ's attitude toward His children . . . one of joy flowing completely.

The atmosphere of heaven is described as "joy in the presence of God and His angels." Worship is to be held in an atmosphere of joy. Psalms 5:11 says:

"But let all those that put their trust in thee rejoice: let them ever shout for joy, because thou defendest them: let them also that love thy name be joyful in thee."

Psalms 63:5b:

". . . and my mouth shall praise thee with joyful lips."

Psalms 63:7:

"Therefore in the shadow of thy wings will I rejoice."

Deuteronomy 12:7 teaches us that we are to rejoice in all that we put our hands unto. Many times the Scripture teaches us that those who seek the Lord are to rejoice! Probably no place in Scripture is as emphatic of God's attitude toward joy as is expressed in Deuteronomy 28:47-48a:

"Because thou servedst not the Lord thy God with joyfulness and with gladness of heart, for the abuandance of all things . . . therefore shalt thou serve thine enemies."

As a pastor for many years, I never saw anyone become lukewarm or go back on their commitment if they kept the joy of their salvation. This is why God gave such a solemn warning to Israel. Can't you picture the days when the offerings were taken to the Temple? What great joy! Singing, dancing in the streets, expressing great joy as they brought their first fruits to offer to the Lord! Picture then, as time passed and the ritual became routine . . . the original joy was no longer there and the act became only ceremonial. Do you see a parallel in the new Christian, just saved and going to church with great joy, tithing with great joy — witnessing with great joy? Then gradually, perhaps because of the "little foxes" of church gossip, or some imperfection in the life of the pastor, or his family becoming oblivious, or any one of the many defects that can tarnish the brightness of the new life . . . the joy begins to ebb away. How wonderful it would be to be able to immunize all baby Christians against this . . . or at least instruct the new convert in how to rebuke and resist the "little foxes." Anything that takes our joy is not of God and when we lose our joy we are in danger of beginning to serve the enemy and being in spiritual want.

I have had the personal privilege of being a part of the great revival of this era with its exploding churches and expanding pulpits. Churches that have gone from nineteen people to over twenty-eight hundred . . . from seventy-five to over fifteen hundred . . . many churches having over 300% growth. In all of these exploding churches there are four common denominators: a spirit of fellowship, a spirit of worship, a spirit of joy, and a spirit of faith. I have often noticed how quickly these congregations respond with joyful laughter, how their faces beam as they listen to the Word, how quick they are to hug one another with pure joy. This joy flowing is a quick, ready laugh . . . a joy expressed and a flashing smile. They sense the joyful presence of our Lord. He is in their midst. People who all their lives felt rejected now feel accepted by their new brothers and sisters. Drug addiction and other vices have been replaced by the satisfying portion of grace. Marriages that were shipwrecked are now being healed and sailing on a sea of happiness. The body of Christ is coming together in joyful worship. Miracles are happening and God's love flows in the joy of the Lord.

In Acts 8:8, where there was revival, there was great joy in that city after the outpouring of the Holy Ghost. They broke bread from house to house, did eat their meat with gladness (exultation) and singleness of heart.

We will always face many tests . . . but the Lord is our strength. We can be happy if we want to, or we can be miserable if we desire. It is our attitude that will be showing. If you are having difficulty showing a good, positive, happy attitude, then learn how to express good, solid, scripture-based convictions. Let them flow. Speak them out loud:

"I can do all things through Christ."

"Greater is He that is in me than he that is in the world."

"If God be for me who can be against me."

"I can run through a troop and leap over a wall!"

Then expect that attitude to change. Turn the corners of your mouth up instead of down. Don't cry . . . laugh! God is your Father and Jesus is your elder Brother. Amen.

Time to Laugh:

A mother had taken her small son to the toy department of a large downtown store. It was time for them to leave, but the little boy, who was very stubborn and strong-willed, was determined to stay on the rocking horse and play a while. The mother had tried every way she knew to make him mind, being especially mindful of the advice she had had about raising a child without spanking or inhibiting him in any way. The clerks had even tried to bribe him with candy but he wouldn't budge. A well known child psychiatrist just happened by chance to appear and the mother implored him to help her get the little boy off the rocking horse. He walked over, bent down and whispered in the child's ear, and without a moment's hesitation the little boy climbed down and came over and took his mother's hand. She said, "What did you say to him?" The psychiatrist answered, "I told him that if he didn't climb down from there immediately I would break every bone in his stubborn little body."

Chapter II

LAUGH WITH GOD

"He that sitteth in the heavens shall laugh." Psalms 2:4.

Psalms 37:13 also teaches that God does laugh. Although these references seem to carry a connotation of derision or of "laughing at" someone, we must remember that God does not laugh **at** the individual but at his absurdity, not at the fool but at his folly. And when we look at godless men from where God sits, we see the ludicrousness of finite man as he spends his lifetime in rebellion against God. I am sure that all of us believe that our Father does have a sense of humor and Jesus, His Son, also enjoys this characteristic. Certainly we, His children, being His offspring, have also inherited this ability to laugh and to express joy.

David A. Redding says, "Once upon a time many church-goers suspected anything funny was subversive. Yesterday's pilgrim didn't dare to clown and Plymouth squeezed itself into a poker face. We're always photographed saying "cheese" but a Winthrop wouldn't have unlaced a smile even for his heirloom portrait. Those old sobersides really scrambled goodness with solemnity. They weren't as dreadful as we are determined to make them, for they knew where frivolity leads. But the Calvinist was so afraid of fun's consequences that he tried, at his fanatic worst, to wipe off every smile, put a stop to dancing and turn off the organ music. He wouldn't let artists play with color on canvas or in stained glass any more . . . so that the Apostles looked as dead pan as cigar store Indians."

Critics unjustly trace to Jesus the depressing graveyard atmosphere that sometimes haunts the Church. The men who really killed joy wore pointed three-cornered hats and buckled shoes. "The parsonical voice, the thin damp smell of stone," as British architect Hugh Casson calls it, were flung like a pall over the faith by some of Cromwell's men. Frankly, this grinning generation doesn't respect its forefathers enough, but those grim graybeards do deserve the blame for taking the fun out of religion.

Christ simply was not cut from black cloth no matter how the Pharisees dressed Him down. The Gospels give us a warm friend, full of life, laughter, and such good news it showered radiance on the head of saint and sinner alike.

It was the Pharisees, long-faced, fasting and frowning, who always appeared to be in perpetual mourning. Christ's men behaved like a feasting bridal party. "How," He asked those who scourned His merrymaking, "can men fast when the bridegroom is still with them?" There is much more to Christianity than skipping along blithely, but neither can it keep always in marked military step. Men may only stand up for the "Hallelujah Chorus," but it makes hearts skip with excitement. Christ was born in a burst of angelic "Joy to the World." And when He came back triumphant from the fight with death, there was such heavenly light, such overwhelming evidence of His resurrection life shining about Him, that men trembled in ecstasy.

This article so ably sets the scene for Christian living that being able to laugh would be, as the youth culture puts it, "making the scene." Being able to laugh with God denotes a joy that is expressed because of our position with Him. Having received Christ, His Son, we are lifted up into heavenly places in Christ Jesus.

"And hath raised us up together and made us sit together in heavenly places in Christ Jesus." Ephesians 2:6.

This is a faith laughter that stems from deep-rooted faith in the finished work of the cross. We are already in God's plan, seated there with His Son, Jesus. The battle is over. The victory is won. We are already victors, wearing the victor's crown. We do not wait to express joy on that final day, but by faith see ourselves there with joy that knows no measure. To rejoice with joy unspeakable is to see ourselves in His presence. Proverbs 10:22 speaks of the blessing of the Lord that maketh rich and addeth no sorrow with it. Zephaniah 3:17 suggests that God is not only mighty but will rejoice over us with joy, and laughter is joy overflowing. He sees us there in His presence, and we see ourselves there by faith. When the disciples saw their risen Lord and knew it was He they had with them, the Scripture states "they believed it not for joy." Or, what they really said was, "it's too good to be true." Joy filled their hearts to even let themselves think of the power and the awesomeness of Christ being raised from the dead. When we, like them, really permit ourselves to see the completeness of redemption, our hearts too shall be so overcome with joy that we could say, "this is too good to be true." Yet, praise God, it is true. We are redeemed, set free and already there in His sight. We can laugh with God, by faith, as we receive this great truth.

"Therefore the redeemed of the Lord shall return and come with singing unto Zion; and everlasting joy shall be upon their head. They shall obtain gladness and joy and sorrow and mourning shall flee away." Isaiah 51:11.

The redeemed come in with singing. This spirit of rejoicing is our heritage. Let us claim this spirit of joy and laughter and, by faith, practice it now. It must cause some commotion before the throne to have an angel announce to the Father that some of His children are on their way with their mouths filled with laughter. If the Father were to ask, "Why?" the angel could reply, "They are anticipating what awaits them when they arrive."

Being able to laugh with God also suggests that we are acquainted with His promises. Yes, there are thousands of them given to us to meet every need and to fit every occasion. The next time a need arises, don't confess the disheartening circumstances with which you are surrounded, but rather quote one of the promises and laugh at the situation that comes against you.

One of the most trying things that most people face is their great concern for loved ones, especially when the loved ones do not seem to respond to prayer and witnessing, but instead seem to become more lethargic and spiritually unresponsive. What is a believer supposed to do in such a case? First of all, saturate your heart and mind with Acts 16:31,

"Believe on the Lord Jesus Christ and thou shalt be saved and thy house."

If it is your children, then do the same with Jeremiah 31:16, 17:

"Thus saith the Lord; Refrain thy voice from weeping, and thine eyes from tears: for thy work shall be rewarded saith the Lord; and they shall come again from the land of the enemy."

Thus, faith seeks the promises of God as God states them, not as you see progress, or the lack of it. This means that even if they confess the Lord and seem to be making progress, you yet see the promise and not the progress! This will safeguard you from having "yo-yo" faith . . . for your faith and confidence is in the Word. God said it, you say it, and that is the way it is going to be. Because of this, faith can laugh with God. It looks down from the position of God's throne on the final page that only He (and you by faith) can see. As someone said, "We have read the last chapter and we win!"

To be able to "laugh with God" suggests that you are one of His children. Israel's behavior identified them as the devil's progeny and Jesus said to them, "You are of your father the devil." Living in a joyful, happy posture signifies that you belong to God. The wealth of His kingdom is yours right now, not in the sweet by and by. Act like it . . . talk like it . . . laugh like it.

Down through the years many have taught wrongly, leaving the impression that God sits on His throne with a great, heavy mallet delighting to "bop" anyone on the head who "deserves" it, with fire, tornadoes, wrecks, dread diseases, etc. They have done such a good job of this teaching that the insurance companies have picked it up and, if you will notice on most insurance contracts, they will not pay on many of these disasters, calling them "acts of God."

It is time to reverse this teaching. It is time to begin to think of our God as a loving Father. As a Psalmist so ably put it,

"Blessed be the Lord God, the God of Israel, who only doeth wondrous things."   Psalms 72:18.

This is not the picture of a God who sits on the throne thinking of ignoble things to do to His children . . . but of the kind, heavenly Father we know He is.

Time to Laugh:

Once upon a time there was an elderly couple who, all of their married lives, had spent their days in argument and dissension . . . which ended in a season of strained silence. One evening, during one of the silent periods, they were sitting on the front porch and saw a team of oxen pulling a wagon. The wife remarked, "See how that team of oxen gets along so well, pulling that load together? Why can't we do that?" Her husband answered, "We could too if we only had one tongue between us."

Chapter III

LAUGHING AT THE DEVIL

"Yahweh" you laugh at them, you make fun of these pagans. — (Jerus.) Psalms 59:8. Yes, God laughs at the enemy, so we can laugh at him. Perhaps one of the most effective weapons of faith in our arsenal is the ability to laugh at Satan. If God can laugh at him from His strength in having conquered him, so also can we! We have cringed before him. He has terrorized us, driven us to great depth of fear, tantalized and taunted us. He has made us question our faith, our Bible, our walk with God, and all of the time he was only a roaring lion with all of his teeth pulled. We have permitted him to defeat us in prayer, defeat us in our home, cause lasting splits in the church, drive us from the ministry and make us worry ourselves into sickness, and all of the time he was a vanquished, defeated foe. We have permitted him to challenge us to try and cast him out. Some have even recorded on tape so-called arguments they lost with him! We let him discourage us in our giving, telling us that we are not better off for having given that 10%. We have let him make us believe his lying symptoms when the Word declared we were healed, and all of those literally millions of times he was only blowing hot air, empty talk, and false accusations! All this time we had only to sit back and laugh at him.

There is no greater evidence of our faith expressed before Satan than to laugh in his face. He can tolerate your promises, dodge your rebukes, leave for a season and return later. But he can't stand your laughter. He can sit by and listen to your prayers of unbelief. He can endure your threats because you don't carry them out. But when you laugh at him, this is new; he is not used to this. What is this laughter coming from the children of God? Where did they learn this? In six thousand years he has heard this so seldom that he stops and listens, for those who dare to laugh at him must certainly know what they are doing or they wouldn't dare laugh at him! "Why, can't they know who I am? I cause nations to tremble; I destroy whole governments and cause them to retire in shame. I ably afflict little children and the strongest men alike. I cause armies to slaughter each other. I cause a man to take up a gun and murder his own wife and children! Who dares to laugh at me? I challenge angels on their way to deliver a message. I go before the courts of heaven and disrupt proceedings. Who dares to laugh at me?" Only those who know they are redeemed by the blood of Jesus Christ, God's only Son; those who know their names are written in the Lamb's Book of Life; those who not only know the power of the Scriptures but can ably quote them in any given situation or emergency; only those who have the power of the Holy Spirit in their lives . . . yes, who know what belongs to them and also know that this homewrecker, rapist of the innocent, and liar of all eternity is nothing but a defeated foe who can only make empty threats and roar in the distance at these redeemed children of God.

Yes, we can laugh at this feared enemy because he is no longer god in our kingdom. We can laugh at him because we have been translated from his kingdom of darkness into the kingdom of God's dear Son (Colossians 1:13). We have a different citizenship, better passports, perfect security. We have changed governments and have a new King . . . His name is Jesus. He is eternal, He is immortal, King of Kings and Lord of Lords. His kingdom is one of light and not darkness. His kingdom is one of love and not hate, one of healing and not suffering. When we realize who we are . . . joint heirs with the heir of all ages, one who has given us His own name, His own power and His own authority, one who has blessed us with all spiritual blessings in heavenly places in Christ Jesus . . . we will not struggle to laugh; it will flow naturally. It will be a laughter of faith that doesn't operate on how we feel, but who we are!

"When the Scripture teaches that God laughs, He is not laughing at peoples' failures, but at their folly." — Jack Hayford. Even atheistic nations reveal their folly when they say they can pull God from His throne. This laughter from God will cause a similar chuckle in all our hearts when we stop to realize this is utter senseless folly.

The story is told about the first Russian cosmonaut. When he returned from the first journey into space he said, "I looked around for God and didn't see Him." One of the American reporters was heard to remark, "If he had stepped out of his space ship he would have."

Laughter at Satan is not recommended for new baby Christians or weak saints. A very well-known Bible College professor remarked, "I wouldn't laugh at the devil because I am afraid he would get mad." This remark, I trust, was made "in jest," because if anyone should know his position in Christ, it ought to be one who teaches the Word. My friend, there may be several reasons why you shouldn't laugh at Satan, but don't worry about making him angry. He has been angry a long time, or haven't you noticed?

This chapter is written to encourage you first of all to learn to know who you are in Christ. Study carefully the following, then you too can laugh at the devil, the defeated one. Remember the words to the chorus sung by so many: "He signed the deed with His atoning blood. He ever lives to make His promise good. Should all the hosts of hell march in to make a second claim, they would all march out at the mention of His name." Ephesians 2:19-22 tells us:

"Thus you are strangers and foreigners no longer, you share the membership of the saints, you belong to God's own household, you are a building that rests on the apostles and prophets as its foundation, with Christ Jesus as the cornerstone; in Him the whole structure is welded together and rises into a sacred temple in the Lord, and in Him you are yourselves built into this to form a habitation for God in the Spirit." Moffatt.

Let us stop to think of a redeemed saint of the household of God, one who bears the name of King Jesus, one whose total inheritance is worth more than all of the world put together, one who has a name on his lips so powerful that if measured by megations, would dwarf all hydrogen bombs . . . whose name someday all will bow before . . . this name, Jesus. That name that causes demons to tremble. To even consider for a minute saints cowering before that defeated enemy is unthinkable. Rather, think of the enemy in full retreat and stand your blood-bought ground, purchased with heaven's sacrifice, and laugh at the devil.

Pastor Bill Popejoy of Belton, Missouri, is known for his delightful whimsical way of stating things. Yet he has gone through some deep waters. He told of a time when he faced surgery for cancer of the throat. As he prayed, it seemed the devil said to him, "You're going to die!" In response he sensed the Holy Spirit said to him, "Goody!", reminding him that this would mean heaven. Then the tempter said, "You're going to lose your voice." Again came the answer of the Spirit, "I've given you a ministry of writing." Once more the attack came, "You'll become deformed." And the delightful answer was, "look in the mirror." Then Pastor Popejoy gave his version of a Bible verse, "Laugh at the devil and he will flee from you." A laugh a day will keep the devil away.

It's real maturity when a person has learned to laugh at life and at himself and to trust in God. **Assembly Lines** by Ralph W. Harris.

Time to Laugh:

A new pastor was invited to join the local Kiwanis Club. The membership secretary reminded him, however, that they were only allowed to have one representative of each profession, and they already had a pastor. The only position not represented right then was that of hog caller. Would the pastor mind? The pastor replied, "Where I came from I was known as a shepherd . . . but of course, you know your group best."

Chapter IV

LEARN TO LAUGH AT (WITH) YOURSELF

"Although the fig tree shall not blossom, neither shall fruit be in the vines; the labour of the olive shall fail and the fields shall yield no meat; the flock shall be cut off from the fold and there shall be no herd in the stalls; yet I will rejoice in the Lord, I will joy in the God of my salvation."   Habakkuk 3:17 & 18.

This beautiful confession of trust that overcomes devastation states so perfectly the Christian's walk of faith. When all else fails, the child of God rejoices. He has joy (laughter) flowing because the Christion joy does not have its basis in that which succeeds or what fails, in shortages, difficulties or negative news reports, but in his salvation which is of God. Oh, yes, you can be as most people "under the circumstances" and talk negatively right along with the rest of the world . . . go on an everlasting "pity party," and seek sympathy. Or you can follow the trend of most theologians and say, "I guess God is trying to teach me something or humble me . . . or expose a weakness in my life by this punishment." Or, you can have the kind of confession that rejoices in Him regardless of what happens in the world! According to W. E. Vine, the word "confess" comes from the Greek word "homologeo" which means "to speak the same thing," "homo" meaning "same" and "logeo" meaning "to speak." Thus, the Christian's confession of faith does not depend on outward circumstances. It doesn't change with the times and conditions but remains the same, saying the same things. Thus the Christian's joy and laughter remains unchanged, saying in all circumstances the same statements of faith, neither going by feelings, nor how things are falling out, whether pleasant places or trying times. He, the child of God, is fixed; he remains the same. He confesses, he laughs, he shouts for joy . . . for it is coming from within, not without. Jesus endured the cross for the joy that was set before Him. The cross did not take His joy . . . neither can circumstances take ours.

You can laugh if you want to. I recall that as a small boy my sister and I would play a game called, "let's get tickled." We discovered a great truth in this simply-contrived game. We would begin to make ourselves laugh even though there was nothing to laugh about (it was during the depression, so there was really very little to cause laughter), and we would begin slowly with first one chuckling and then the other, gradually working up until we were both in a paroxysm of laughter! It was so enjoyable that we did it rather often. You can do the same thing; you can laugh, or you can cry! Sometimes you hear someone tell about an incident that happened years ago and they will say, "I can laugh about it now, but it was no laughing matter then!" Perhaps it would have been better to have laughed about it then, by faith, than to have saved it until now. It would have brightened up all those years in between . . . and perhaps even lengthened your life span because he who laughs takes good medicine that doesn't dry up the bones . . . but rather strengthens them.

One of our pastors relates an incident that illustrates this so very well. He tells of how things in his church were going badly, so badly that he just didn't feel like going on. One day he said to his wife, "I guess what I need is a good laugh." She believed him instantly and began to laugh aloud and tickle him until he was helpless with laughter. Just that simple exercise lifted his spirit and he felt then like going on. Yes, laughter is compared to good medicine because, "A merry heart doeth good like a medicine." It certainly won't hurt. Try it; you'll like it, I'm sure.

We take ourselves so seriously. We bemoan the way we are made; we chafe under the load we carry. Laughter, especially when we learn to laugh at ourselves, frees us from laboring under the criticism of others. Why should I permit how others accept me to be a heavy load on my shoulders? How embarrassed we were as children when someone laughed and poked fun at the way we dressed. What release it would have been to have been taught to laugh with them! If they said, "What an ugly dress," and began to ridicule, you could have said, "Yes, it is kinda funny, isn't it?" When you missed that question in class and all began to tee-hee and giggle, you could have freed yourself of many future scarred years by laughing with them. But we weren't taught that way. I can recall so many embarrassing incidents as a child, some of them leaving a lasting deep impression on my soul. Oh! That someone would have preached a sermon on self-acceptance and release like this, then I could have been taught to laugh at myself. As one young woman said about a friend, "I can't take him seriously until he takes himself more lightly."

A ham actress was belittling the late Marie Dressler's comedy. "What dignity is there to making people laugh?" She squeaked, "I make them cry." Miss Dressler retorted, "Any onion can do that." — **Gordon Gamack.**

Someone has suggested that there are three degrees of laughter. The lowest is the laughter of a man who laughs only at his own jokes; next is the laughter of the man who laughs at the jokes of others. But the highest and finest of all is the laughter of the man who laughs at himself, for this shows the precious ability to look at oneself objectively. If we can do that, worries have a comforting habit of diminishing in importance . . . to mere nuggets.

It was once remarked to Lord Chesterfield that man is the only creature endowed with the power of laughter. "True," said the peer, "and you may add, perhaps that he is the only creature that deserves to be laughed at." — **Canning Trade.**

Laughter is the chorus of conversation. — Philnems. The people of the world seem to know the value of laughter and they enjoy it . . . but theirs is a laughter that only happens when something occurs to make it happen. The joy that flows in laughter, without anything occurring to make it happen, is a joy that shows its eternal freedom by expressing itself despite outward circumstances. It is the joy given by our Lord Jesus. We are a new creature, a new creation. Eternal joy is evidence of our citizenship and laughter is the passport.

Sadness and its expressions are of a fallen race of people who have no hope. Frowns show displeasure in yourself and to others, and gloom and sadness will fill hell's atmosphere. No laughter there, no joy there. Teach your mouth to express your born-again heart . . . laugh when you don't feel like it, even if you have to look in the mirror to get it started. Learning to laugh at yourself may take some time, so why not begin now?

Time to Laugh:

The story is told about a young minister who was sent to fill the pulpit of a vacationing pastor. As he drove up to the church he saw that one of the window. panes had been broken out and a piece of cardboard was placed there to keep out the weather. He said to himself, "I guess I am like that cardboard, just placed here temporarily to keep out the weather." In the course of his message that morning, he referred to himself as that piece of cardboard. One of the parishoners, thinking to compliment the young man, remarked on the way out, "You are not like that piece of cardboard, you are a real pane."

Chapter V

THE WHOLE MAN REJOICES

Proverbs 17:22:

"A merry heart doeth good like a medicine; but a broken spirit drieth the bones."

"A rejoicing heart doeth good to the body."   YLT

"A joyful heart worketh an excellent cure."   RHM

"A cheerful heart makes a quick recovery."   Knox

According to Dr. Ern Crocker of Sydney, Australia, those who find it easy to laugh seldom have heart attacks. Surely this scripture can be believed and acted upon. If so, this one ought to be a favorite of all Christians.

As a pastor of many years experience, I never visited a sick person and found him laughing. A marriage counsellor has yet to have a troubled couple come into his office laughing. How many very tense moments have been broken by one party suddenly laughing? God intended laughter to be a way of life for His people.

"And the very God of peace sanctify you wholly; and I pray God your whole spirit, and soul and body be preserved blameless unto the coming of our Lord Jesus Christ."   I Thessalonians 5:23.

This scripture teaches not only that we are tri-partate in nature, but that each part is to be in right relationship . . . even each part whole and sanctified.

There is a part that the body plays, the soul plays, and also a part which the spirit plays. This wholeness, this healing, is lacking in so many of the Lord's people. The very fact that so many say, "body, soul and spirit," instead of the Biblical, "spirit, soul, and body," bears out this misunderstanding. Inasmuch as many books are written on this subject, it is not my intention to do a special treatise, but rather to point out the proper relationship each will play in order to contribute to the completeness of the whole man.

The subject of the body is best understood in its positive role rather than its negative. Inasmuch as the body cannot sin by itself, or act independently, suggests that most of our time should be given to discussing the soul and spirit. The body is the tabernacle, the house for the inner man or the eternal man. It is a temple for the Holy Spirit. The body obeys those signals it receives from the five senses of the soul and spirit. Romans 12:1, . . . the body presented a living sacrifice in worship, is sufficient as a definition at this time. The body "under control" not "controlling."

The soul, the seat of the emotions, will and intellect, is where and from where we have our earthly existence. It is the "real us" . . . our personalities, our likes, dislikes, etc. When we are born again, it is our spirit, dead in trespasses and sins, that is made alive unto God. Thus the new creature is being formed. If, after this experience takes place, we are yet controlled by the same old soulishness, then we will yet be carnal and not much change will be evident. Our souls must be influenced by our new spirits and hearts which are from God. Old things must pass away. According to I Peter 2:1, we must lay aside malice, guile, hypocrisy, envyings and all evil speaking, vain conversations received by traditions. The soul and its emotions must change if we are to receive benefits from the born-again spirit.

Jesus said in John 15:11:

". . . that my joy might remain in you (spirit) that your joy (soul emotions) might be full."

Thus the joy and redemption (born-again spirit) must be expressed by the soul through the body. You can express how you feel from your soulish realm and it will be the same as when you were in your lost condition. When you make yourself express the joy of your born-again heart (spirit), you then express the joy, through your soul, that Christ gives. The joyful sound is here, it is happiness, it is laughter. Thus it is the joy of the Lord that is our strength. It is this joy that comes from the well of salvation . . . the joy that no man can take (John 16:22).

The whole man, standing before the Lord, expresses himself in many ways. When I bow my head to reverence Him, my bowed head is saying, "My whole nature bows before You." When I lift up my hands in worship, my lifted hands say, "My soul and my spirit worship You." And when you hear me clap my hands in joy, my whole tri-partate nature is expressing joy. Often we hear folks say, "I am not as others. I can't express what I feel." Perhaps they have inherited a very introverted nature from their parents. They need to be reminded that they now have a new Father. They need to make their bodies respond to that new-found joy in Christ and in salvation.

Jesus said your joy might be full. The Amplified Version reads, "that your joy and gladness may be full measure and complete and overflowing." Overflowing joy will come out as laughter just as overflowing sorrow comes out as crying. We all know that the physical body responds to the soulish emotions.

That is why medical science teaches us that up to 90% of all our sicknesses are psychosomatically induced. In the part of the country where I was brought up, we branded some people as being whiners, or some might have been called complainers, always whining or always complaining. It has become a way of life to them. They could change if they wanted to and become joyful. Perhaps some of them need to become converted by receiving Christ. If they do, one of the characteristics ought to be joy.

Food experts can recommend all types of diets to aid the human body in thwarting sickness . . . fat free diets, vitamins, health foods, nature foods, protein, carbohydrates . . . all types, shapes and sizes of packaged advice. But then we notice the expert in diets dies of a heart attack. Probably it is best summarized by saying, "It is not what you eat, but what is eating you." All medical experts agree to this: It is tension, anger, resentment, jealousy, fear, stress and worry that eat away at our source of strength. We allow everyday living conditions to upset us and we allow other people to transfer their problems to us.

The author recalls a time when a person came to him with a problem. He looked like he had a serious one, downcast and dejected. I said, "I will be glad to help you if I can," and then braced myself for what I thought would surely be a spinechiller of a problem. He instead related this problem: he was very good and generous to some friends, loaning them his car, taking them out to dine and having them over to his house for meals. I then said, "What is your problem?" He replied, "These people never return the favor; they never take me out; don't offer me the use of their cars; don't invite me to their homes." I said, "If you are doing the right thing in giving and they are not reciprocating, who has the problem, you or them?" He thought about this for a moment, then brightness filled his face as he said, "I guess they do." "That's right," he said, "I don't have a problem, do I?"

But how many times we allow other people to transfer their hangups to us. We drive down the street and some foolish driver cuts us off or almost bangs into us. We blow the horn, hurl insults, get uptight, tell him off . . . even though he can't hear. Yes, we certainly give them a piece of our minds . . . a (peace) of our minds that we will never get back. The next door neighbors have a big brawl. You listen in and get upset. They are having a big fight and just dragged you into it. Small children get into a hassle and involve moms and dads. The kids are soon friends, but have transferred their problem to moms and dads who never speak to each other again, sometimes even moving out of the neighborhood to try to get away from a problem that they only take with them.

A merry heart doeth good. Take a dose, laugh it away . . . don't let others give you their problems. Help people if you can, but say, "That's your problem, reckless driver; that's your problem, unhappy customer; that's your problem, old world, not mine. I refuse to let you give it to me."

Adam Clarke says of Nehemiah 8:10, "Religious joy, properly tempered with continual dependence on the help of God, meekness of mind, and self-deference, is a powerful means of strengthening the soul. In such a state every duty is practicable, and every duty delightful. In such a frame of mind no man ever fell, and in such a state of mind the general health of the body is much improved; a cheerful heart is not only a continual feast, but also a continual medicine."

A joyful heart is an excellent cure . . . makes you have a quick recovery. Believe God's Word. Have a merry heart, a singing heart, a forgiving heart, a soft heart . . . break those tensions, worries and fears with a peal of laughter. You can do it if you want to.

Time to Laugh:

The pastor's wife wanted a new chandelier for the entryway of the church. The pastor brought it up at the next council meeting. After due deliberation the church council made this decision. "We can't have it for four reasons. First, we can't afford it. Second, nobody can spell it. Third, even if we did get it, nobody could play it . . . and fourth, what we really need is more light!"

Chapter VI

FAITH CAN LAUGH

When one thinks or studies about faith, he must include Abraham, the father of faith. According to James 2:23, he was also called "friend of God." Father of faith or friend of God is as great a compliment as was ever bestowed on a mortal man.

His title of "father of faith" comes as a result of being the first person to walk by faith. To venture out into a place he had never been or seen through simple obedience is a prime example of walking in faith. He didn't need a map; he didn't need to spy out the land; he didn't need to talk with anyone who had already been there. He received his marching orders and obeyed, and thus became the father of not only Israel, but of all who would ever follow and believe as he did.

"Know ye therefore that they which are of faith, the same are the children of Abraham."   Galatians 3:7.

So he is not only the father of faith to the Jew but also to all Christian believers. All the blessings that came upon Abraham will also come on all who are of faith.

"So then they which be of faith are blessed with faithful Abraham."   Galatians 3:9.

We need to examine very carefully the walk and life of this man of faith. God honored him, blessed him and heard and answered his prayers. He blessed him in peace and in time of war and prospered him until he had not one need, being one of the wealthiest men to ever live.

First, let us see how his faith worked for him and then we shall examine his personality. The book of Genesis gives us a detailed record of what happened. Romans 4 tells us how it happened. Most everyone who has any Bible knowledge is acquainted with the story of how Sarah, wife of Abraham, was childless and an old woman of 90 when the Lord promised her she would bear a child. Abraham himself was over 100 years old. Romans 4:17 gives us Faith Lesson No. 1. "Calling those things which are not as though they were." God here gives us a mighty thing to confess . . . "those things which are not as though they are!" How does your faith speak? How does your conversation sound in time of great need? Do you talk about things as they are? When you are sick do you talk about your sickness as it is, describing every symptom in detail? Or is your conversation as though you were already made well and rejoicing? From childhood most of us were taught by our parents to get sympathy by not only describing our symptoms, but even exaggerating, so as to hear a sympathetic, "You poor dear, lie down and I'll take care of you." Does this call back any memories to you as you read it? Most of us will sigh and have to admit that we were not only taught this as a child, but that it has carried over into our adulthood and we can still do a good job of sympathy-seeking, negative talking. Have you noticed that people who continually speak confidently and positively seldom get any sympathy? Have you also noticed that they have very little need for it?

How about your finances? Do you talk about what you "do not have?" It is probably the truth, but it is not faith. You could talk about the wealth you will have because God is your father and He will supply your every need. How does your conversation sound when you are laid off your job? Do you hear yourself saying, "I don't know what we are going to do" . . . or, do you hear yourself saying, "God must have a better job for me somewhere"? If your conversation is the latter, then you are calling those things which are not as though they were.

Abraham did this in Romans 4:19:

"And being not weak in faith, he considered not his own body now dead when he was about an hundred years old neither yet the deadness of Sarah's womb."

I heard about a man who had tried everything he knew to receive his healing. Nothing seemed to work. In desperation he determined to believe God, using this verse. He refused to consider his own body and symptoms. When after a time nothing had happened and he was in the same condition as before, he inquired of the Lord saying, "I am lying here and not considering anything and nothing is happening." The Lord said, "That is your problem. You are not considering anything. Why don't you consider me?" He did, and was healed. He turned his thoughts AWAY from all his symptoms and put them ON God. You cannot consider or talk about things as they are and at the same time talk about how they will be by faith. Abraham, the father of faith, knew this and practiced it. Considering and talking about your symptoms will never encourage your faith but rather will destroy it.

Someone has said that if the Railway Expressman delivers a box of rattlesnakes to your door, he cannot leave them unless you sign for them. This simple illustration witnesses that we should not "sign for" or accept or claim anything we do not want. Abraham was not signing for a failure. He refused to accept defeat even when all proof seemed to indicate it.

"He staggered not at the promise of God through unbelief, but was strong in faith giving glory to God."

Romans 4:20.

Unbelief will make you stagger — reel with uncertainty — say things you should not say. Unbelief expressed takes authority in your heart and reigns in your emotions.

Abraham had every right to sit down and have a long pity party for himself, but instead he praised the Lord, gave glory to Him and believed in Him against all odds. That is exactly how your faith will work for you. Thank God for a thing before you get it, as you would after you received it! Anyone can give glory and thank God for it after they receive it, but faith expresses appreciation before it happens. You can almost hear our Father say to an angel, "What is it that Abraham is so happy about?" The angel would reply, "He is thanking you for the son you are going to give him in his old age." The Father's response would be, "Well then, it must be time to bring it to pass."

What do you need? Have you asked for it? Have you thanked Him for it? Yes! Thank Him now for it to the extent that when you receive it you will not have to say a thing, because you will have already said it! What kind of man is this man of faith? First he was a "friend of God." Faith is not a gimmick or gadget fashioned to get things from God. Your faith will build a beautiful relationship with God. How many friendships are based only on what one party received, but never himself gives? Abraham gave as much as he received . . . "giving glory to God."

Abraham also had another great principle in his personality that all of us should emulate. He had a great sense of humor. When God informed him that they were to have a son in their old age, Abraham laughed so hard he fell on his face. Genesis 17:17. Not only did he have a great sense of humor, but Sarah did also for she laughed, not in unbelief as some might think, because Hebrews 11:11 tells us she had faith to have the strength to have a child. Yes, this family, the first family of faith, gives us this great example that faith can laugh and does, indeed, laugh. In fact, they laughed so much that they named their son "Laughter," which is the meaning of the name "Isaac."

Laughter is joy overflowing. E. Merrill Roots says, "Laughter is the outward sign of inward and invisible freedom." Even in times when all symptoms say "no," the body feels negative, friends and neighbors are discouraging, medical reports are disheartening . . . then faith looks over the whole picture and laughs because it can see the results.

Time to Laugh:

A young man, called to pastor a small church in New England and attending his first service, found only one man in attendance. He asked the man's opinion as to whether they should go ahead and have a service. The man replied, " Well, if I take a load of hay down to feed the cattle and only cow shows up, I feed her." So the young man went through every exercise of the service from beginning to end and when it was finished he asked the man, "How was it?" The man replied, "Well, I'll tell you, when I take a load of hay down to feed the cattle and only one cow shows up, I don't feed her the whole load."

Chapter VII

HEARING YOURSELF LAUGH

"Blessed is the people that know the joyful sound."

Psalms 89:15.

The word "blessed," according to the Amplified Translation, means "happy, fortunate, and to be envied." Laughter can be described as "joy flowing." People who know the joyful sound are people who hear themselves laugh, because joy is something the psalmist described as having sound. When you put sound to joy . . . it comes out laughter!

While the world and the people of the world can laugh, their laughter usually depends on outward circumstances and on what happens. The child of God is supposed to have the joy of the Lord under all circumstances (John 15:11). Hebrews 3:17 teaches that when the shortages get so bad that nothing is left, the child of God will have joy . . . and joy flowing is laughter.

I recall a statement a young soldier made who had been in Vietnam for several years. When he was asked what changes he noticed when he returned, he said, "People don't seem to laugh as much as they did when I left." I suppose this lost laughter could be attributed to the day and age in which we live . . . days of tensions, shortages and fear. Israel, the people of God, had also lost their laughter and the joyful sound. Psalms 137 tells a very sad story of this great people who had known all the rich flow of God's blessing. After they were taken captive by the enemy they were asked to sing one of the songs of Zion and they replied, "How shall we sing the Lord's song in a strange land?" or, paraphrased, "How can we be happy while we are in bondage?" However, Psalms 126 tells us that when they were delivered, "Then was their mouth filled with laughter and their tongue with singing." Lost laughter by a child of God indicates the possibility of some kind of bondage or discouragement.

Having served as a pastor for many years, I discovered that young people usually betray their spiritual condition, relation and walk with the Lord Jesus by their outward show of happiness or by their lack of joy. People who are easily discouraged in their inner man usually can't keep it from showing in their countenance. "Blessed are the people who know the joyful sound" would indicate that it is as important for you to hear yourself laughing as it is for God to hear your expression. For when you hear yourself, even if you have to force it, that very sound coming from within you sounds on your inner ear and speaks very loudly to your inner man.

Jesus said in Mark 4:24,

"Take heed what you hear: with what measure ye mete, it shall be measured to you, and unto you that hear shall more be given."

Strong's Concordance uses the word "estimate," or "importance" could be used; that is, if you value that which you hear, the very value you place on it shall be given back to you in the same measure by which you valued it.

Most of us know that we have an outer ear and an inner ear. We hear sounds from outside by our outer ear and we hear ourselves speak or laugh by the inner ear. That is why the first time you hear yourself on a tape recorder you don't sound like you do when you hear yourself speaking or laughing. When you hear yourself speaking negatively by your inner ear, you are defeating yourself; you are not giving yourself a chance to rise above the circumstances. What you hear yourself saying vibrates off your inner ear bone structure and makes a great impact on your inner man which, in turn, feeds to your whole system of nerves and blood vessels. Besides this, you must be placing great value on what you are saying because you are hearing it, and Jesus said take heed what you hear. Since one can't stop what he hears on the outer ear (and no one can unless he wears ear muffs), he must have been referring to the inner ear. Over this you have complete control. Place high value on what you hear yourself saying, for Jesus promised that more would be given to them who valued what they heard. The Greek work "prostithemi" simply means a continuous action. Expressing joy or laughter has a great effect on the inner ear, thus, the whole man receives a healing dose of good medicine. Stop serving yourself the gall of sorrow and serve joy.

The greatest value to be gained by hearing yourself in your inner ear are those statements that will offset the sickness caused by and coming through your subconscious mind. A mother went to a doctor concerning her physical problems. After a complete examination the doctor couldn't find anything organically wrong. After questioning her he found that her physical problems began after her son had been arrested for dealing in drugs. What could she have done to have offset this terrible news that she heard? If she were a child of God, she should have immediately heard herself saying, "Praise God for Romans 8:28. Thank you, Lord, for dealing with my son; deal firmly with him, Lord, for we have done all we can do and we rest on and will trust you to work out this situation."

Another young girl about to be married came down with rheumatoid arthritis. After much suffering and many sessions of counseling, it was discovered that she dreaded marrying her boyfriend because of a terrible home situation as a child. How can we teach even our children to overcome problems thrust upon them by environmental conditions? Teach them the Scriptures, teach them to sing, teach them how to create their own environment by saying good things in their own ears. You might say, "I wish I had known these things as a child; when I heard Mom and Dad quarrelling I could have said, 'Jesus loves me and I will have a happy home when I marry'." You would have then and there offset those negatives. You might say, "Is it too late?" No, a thousand times, no. Begin now and sound off in your inner ear by opening your mouth and saying good things, scriptural and wholesome words . . . the best sound being the joyful one, that of mirth and laughter.

Hearing the joyful sound would also indicate that you know the benefits, the blessedness of this sound. Psalms 5:11:

"But let all these that put their trust in thee rejoice: let them ever shout for joy, because thou defendest them: let them also that love thy name be joyful in thee."

When we lose our joy we say to ourselves, "I no longer trust God to be my defender for, if I believe that He is my defense, then I will shout for joy!" This is lifting up my voice in victory because I know even ahead of time what the outcome will be. This particular psalm also shows that when I make myself rejoice I love His name. If I don't rejoice and I lose my joy, do I really love His name? If His name means something to me I will be joyful and rejoice . . . my ears will hear the joyful, blessed sound.

If you have lost your laughter, your relationship with your Lord may be suffering. Check your spiritual condition and get help if you need it. Restore the relationship, tear down the dam and let the joy flow.

Time to Laugh:

The story is told about a man who was traveling abroad. He couldn't find the right gift to send his mother. Finally he saw a very beautiful, exotic bird that could sing and also talk. My, he thought, just the right gift and it will also keep Mom company. After he had mailed the bird to her he phoned long distance to see how she was enjoying her present. "Mom, how was the gift I sent you?" The answer was, "Very delicious." After a moment of shocked silence he said, "You ate it? That was a trained talking bird!" She said, "Oh my . . . why didn't it say something then!!"

Chapter VIII

JOY BRINGS DELIVERANCE

Acts 16:16-40 brings to us a delightful story of the power of joy released in the midst of a most trying and difficult circumstance. Paul and Silas were sent out as missionaries to the heathen. This is never easy under the best of conditions but this was particularly hazardous because the Roman laws forbade the introduction of new religions other than that which was already publicly permitted. For this reason the Jews were banished from Rome and Socrates was condemned. The law stated:

> "No person shall have any separate gods, nor new ones, nor shall he privately worship any strange gods, unless they be publicly allowed."   — Adam Clark.

As Paul and Silas ministered in Philippi, a demon possessed girl, who was controlled by men who used her nefariously for gain in divination and soothsaying, began to follow them crying aloud, "These men are the servants of the most High God . . .". After many days of this Paul turned to her and demanded the spirit to come out of her in the name of Jesus Christ. When the wicked men saw that their source of income was cut off, they incensed the crowd against the missionaries and caused them to be beaten severely and cast into prison. We can now describe a very terrible condition under which no average person could rejoice.

The Jews had a law that a man could not receive over thirty lashes with the whip. The Romans had no such law. Paul and Silas were cruelly beaten and thrown, near death, into a clammy, dark, cold dungeon where their hands and feet were securely fastened to the stone wall. Here is a testing ground under the direst of circumstances. How does the average believer react in a suitation such as this . . . though few are this severely tried? We can almost hear the remarks of many, "Why, God, why did this have to happen to me?" . . . "I have sacrificed, left home and family, and look what I get!" "Doesn't God take care of His own?" or, "I must be out of God's will!" Some even blame their misfortune on the ones back home for not praying for them, launching out on a "pity party."

Let's imagine the conversation as the average Christian would have pictured it, that might have taken place between Paul and Silas after they became conscious. "Paul, are you there?" "Yes . . . hurts, doesn't it?" "Yes." "You're not very talkative, Silas." "I know. I was thinking . . . where do you think we missed it?" "I'm not sure, Silas, perhaps we should have gone on into Asia." "But Paul . . . the Spirit forbade us to go." "I thought so too, but maybe we missed it." "Well, perhaps we are to be among those whom God has chosen to suffer and die for Him." This is a picture of what would have transpired in the dungeon if the scene was reconstructed in the imagination of the average Christian.

If we look again at the account given of this incident in the Scriptures we can in no way imagine the conversation between these two godly men as we have just written it. Indeed, it must have sounded more like this: "Paul, can you hear me?" "Yes . . . I hear." "What are you thinking, Paul?" "Well, I thought for a few minutes there that we were both going to die and I rejoiced so at the thought that we would soon see Jesus and was happy just thinking about it." "I was thinking the same thing, Paul . . . Hallelujah!" "Silas . . . you sing better than I do, why don't you start us off singing a chorus of praise?" Thus they sang, loud enough that the other prisoners heard them, and the Bible makes it clear that they were singing "praises unto God." There are some who read into this instance that they thanked God "for" the beating. There is a great difference in praising God "in" your trial and thanking God "for" the trial. In Philippians 4:5 the Word teaches "in" everything give thanks. I Thessalonians 5:18 teaches the same . . . TCNT translates it as "under all circumstances give thanks to God." According to Thayer, Ephesians 5:20 could be "giving thanks always **over** all things." These scriptures certainly do not convey the thought of thanking God "for" sickness or accidents. Do not be as a man we heard recently who was misled by this erroneous teaching and stood to give thanks to God "for" the leukemia that was taking his life from him.

The test that Paul and Silas went through was caused by the devil. They certainly didn't thank God for Satan! It simply teaches us that in all circumstances and conditions we are to be happy ad to rejoice. Philippians 4:4. Being joyful (and joy flowing is laughter) does bring supernatural deliverance. God did hear them. God did honor them. He sent a local earthquake that shook the bars and gates . . . and loosed the locks that bound His children. This is the major difference in the earthquakes that God sends and those the devil sends. God's earthquakes save people and the devil's earthquakes destroy people.

Through this incident God saved the jailor and his family, publicly honored his servants, and embarrassed the enemy. Praise and joy expressed will bring God on the scene! How many of God's people down through the years have emulated this great example? How many have expressed worship and praise instead of blame and fault? How many have sung praises to God rather than falling in a bog of self pity, feeling sorry for themselves?

There are many books written which teach us that it is the Christian's lot to go down into the valley of despair . . . that you cannot know the beauty of the mountain top unless you first know the sorrow of the valley. Books that teach you this are wrong. Do not heed their advice. Rather, do as Paul and Silas did. When everything seems to be lost, pray and sing praises to God. Make yourself rejoice.

Many people equate more love and compassion to their earthly parents than they do to God. They do this by believing that it is God who sends the floods, the fire, the sickness, the droughts . . . but they would not for a moment believe that their earthly fathers would put sickness upon them or let them go hungry, let alone cause it! Would an earthly father allow his child to be badly burned to teach it a painful lesson? Would an earthly father cut off the hand of his child to teach the child to more appreciate the other hand? No! We would take such a parent to court and send him to prison. But we constantly blame God for tragedies, forgetting that II Corinthians 4:4 teaches that the god of this world, Satan, is the one who is in control of the weather, floods, fire, famine and pestilence, for he is the prince of this world. The next time you seem to be the victim of one of these onslaughts, remember that you have been translated from the power of darkness to God's kingdom (Colossians 11) and refuse to accept it. Rebuke the devil and boldly proclaim for everyone to hear that you are a child of God. Praise God and make yourself release the joy that is yours. Joy flowing is laughter.

Time to Laugh:

Clyde was one of the unfortunates who seemed singled out to continually walk under a cloud of trouble and misfortune. Nothing he ever did seemed to turn out right. Clyde was a good man . . . went to church, but even that didn't seem to help. His brother never went to church, never pretended to be religious, yet his crops were always big and his farm prosperous! Clyde had tried his hand at many things — and, one by one, they had all failed — until, as a last resort and because he saw his brother doing so well, he decided to try farming. He bought all of his equipment and a plot of land. On his first day out on his new tractor, just as he made the first turn in the field, the tractor overturned, dumping Clyde in the soft mud, coming to rest on top of him. Clyde lay there on his back with his eyes toward heaven in complete dejection and said, "Why, God, why me?" He heard a voice from above saying, "I don't know, Clyde, there's just something about you that ticks me off."

Chapter IX

REJOICE! GOD WILL MEET YOU

Isaiah 64:5. "Thou meetest him that rejoiceth."

Ezekiel 1:16 speaks of a wheel and a wheel in the middle of a wheel . . . describing their appearance and their work. As you read these words you might think them to be the words of Dr. Einstein relating something he saw. But this is the Spirit of God allowing us to see into the spiritual, eternal dimension from the realm of the dimension of time and the physical.

The Bible pictures God as being Light in I John 1:5. The scientists know that light travels at an amazing speed of 186,272 miles per second. This is so exceedingly fast that it travels 6 million million (5.88 trillion) miles in one year. We cannot understand this unless we bring it down to our measure of comprehension. Let us illustrate it thus. If you were to wind up an old-fashioned alarm clock and begin to count the tick-tocks for 32,000 years, you would have a million million. Yet light travels 6 million million miles in one year. In one hour it travels 670,000,000 miles. If you were to fire a rifle whose bullet would travel the speed of light, it would travel around the circumference of the earth over seven times before you could remove your finger from the trigger.

Accepting the fact then that light comes from God, we can say that if one were to begin traveling, accelerating the speed faster and faster, he would begin moving toward the eternal dimension from the time dimension. This is confirmed by the scientists who say that as you accelerate faster and faster, time slows down more and more so that, if you could travel at the speed of light, time would stop. This is called the "time dialation" theory and is based on the Einstein law of relativity which is stated as $E=MC2$. If you were to travel in a space ship at 87% the speed of light, time would slow down 50%. This could be illustrated with the help of a little imagination. Think of yourself in a space ship travelling 87% the speed of light. You could travel into outer space for 20 years, turn your space ship around and return to earth, having been gone a total of 40 years. Imagine your surprise when you stepped out of your space ship and discovered that everyone on earth had aged . . . and those who were your age when you left are now twice as old as you are! If you were to step this up until you are traveling 99.99% the speed of light and traveled into outer space for a total of 60 years, when you returned you would find that 5 million years would have passed while you were gone. Yes, if you could travel at 100% the speed of light, time would stop and the moment now would be forever . . . for that is where God's throne is and where the timeless, eternal dimension exists.

If you are wondering what is faster than light, you may recall that the Lord's return to take us out of this world is going to be in an atomic second. I Corinthians 15:52. King James translates the word "atomo" to "moment" or "twinkling of an eye." The Lord will take us out of this world so fast that time will stop and the moment now will be forever for us. No aging in heaven, no more of time's depredations . . . time will be no more.

Think back with me now to what Ezekiel saw . . . the wheel. Picture in your mind the universe as being a mammoth wheel with the center, or hub, being the location of the throne of God or the eternal dimension, and each spoke reaching out from the hub as one time zone. If you could sit where God sits in the hub, or eternal dimension, you could look out to the rim and see every time zone from the beginning of creation to the end of all things. You could see Adam and Eve in the garden. You could see Noah's day. You could see the glorious night of the birth of the Savior, the dark day of His death, and His triumphant resurrection. You could see the glory and power of the day of Pentecost. You could even look ahead and see the panorama of your life and the day of your death, even the end that God permitted John to see in Revelation 7:9. The last spoke in the great wheel would be when he saw a number that no man could number! Oh, but you say, if he saw me there that would be predestination! No, it is not predestination, but foreknowledge. Because, you see, what you **do** is what God **sees.** If you walk in obedience to His commands, this is what He sees. If you reject the message and walk in your own ways, this is what He sees.

Your faith, God's gift to you (Ephesians 2:8, 9), will work and serve you better as you endeavor to see by faith from the position of God's throne, or the hub, rather than from the time dimension, or the rim. If you see only from the time dimension, you see your problems and troubles. If, by faith, you see from the hub or the eternal dimension, you see as God sees. In II Kings 6:17, all that the young man could see (from the time zone) was their plight in being surrounded by the enemy. When the prophet (seeing from the eternal zone) prayed that his eyes would be opened, the young man then saw what Elisha had already seen — and knew they were surrounded by horses and chariots of fire whom God had sent in their behalf.

Many times what you see . . . what you feel . . . even what you know, causes worry and fear. But begin now to see the daily exercise of your life from God's throne downward. See what He sees. We are surrounded by angels, chariots of fire and thousands of promises.

A story is told by a chaplain of World War II of how his plane was disabled and was coming in with the remaining crew prepared for a crash landing. As the chaplain prayed, his eyes were opened and he saw through the window an angel holding the wing tip of the airplane. One might remark that he too could believe if he could see into the other realm. But a special blessing is pronounced on those who believe even though they don't see. John 20:29. We see by faith. Anyone can be happy when he can see the answer and have already what he needs. But the child of God can be happy because of what God has declared. That is all he needs.

Most of our unbelief is caused by fear. Fear robs us of our faith and our joy. When children of God learn to think from God's throne downward, rather than from our troubled world upward, we begin to see the end result rather than the difficulty with which we are now faced. We see ourselves surrounded by everyday troubles. God sees us before the throne receiving our crowns of righteousness. We see what we think is a bad marriage for loved ones, but God can see the future and see them happy. We see a rebellious teenager and worry ourselves sick, but God sees him not only saved but in the ministry.

You remark, "But what if this doesn't happen?" Then you are seeing only from the time zone, when your faith should be expressing what God can do from the eternal dimension. Laughter will rise up and express itself as you see yourself sitting with Christ in heavenly places. How many saints, even though they died in great physical pain, were laid in their caskets with smiles on their faces because the last thing they saw before they died was the Lord Jesus coming for them? At the last they had a picture from the other side. Why not formulate, by faith, this picture often. See yourself after God has brought you through. Don't see yourself going under, but over . . . not defeated but victorious.

Often when I am in difficulty and don't know which way to turn, I say to God, "What did you see me doing to get out of this?" Many times the wisdom will come and the problem is solved.

Is the Scripture true? Will He meet you if you rejoice? Isaiah 64:5. Yes, He said He would. A rejoicing heart is a singing heart. It is a heart of mirth, not heaviness. It is a heart that rejoices by faith for it sees as God sees . . . a victory, a loved one saved, a ministry fulfilled, a life completed. Rejoice, friend, God will meet you.

Time to Laugh:

There was a mountain climber who fell off the sheer wall of a cliff. As he fell, he managed to grasp a small tree growing from the side of the mountain and clung there precariously as he looked down several thousand feet to the canyon floor. He looked up to the top of the mountain, still several hundred feet distant and called, "Help, is there anyone up there?" The answer came back, "Yes." "Who is it?" "I am Jesus." "Can you help me?" The voice answered, "Yes, but you will have to let go of the tree." A moment's silence, and then, "Is there anyone else up there?"

Chapter X

LEARN TO LAUGH

A baby, by its actions, teaches us that easy laughter is normal. Crying indicates something is wrong. When the child is well rested and fed it laughs and plays easily. A constantly crying child is irritating and brings no joy.

> "For the kingdom of God is not meat and drink; but righteousness and peace, and joy in the Holy Ghost."
>
> Romans 14:17.

> "Righteousness and peace have kissed each other (go together)."
>
> Psalms 85:10.

If circumstances or your enemy can rob you of either one, you lose your joy. Satan can't take your joy unless he disturbs your sense of right-standing with God. When he does this he reminds you of your past sins and failures. As one saint so ably expressed it, "God forgives our sins and puts them in the sea of forgetfulness and puts up a sign that says 'no fishing'." Don't permit Satan to probe into your past. Commit to memory II Corinthians 5:21:

> "For he hath made him to be sin for us, who knew no sin; that we might be made the righteousness of God in him."

Know that your right standing with God is something that God did, and not you. The Greek word for righteousness is "dikaeosune" and literally means "rightwiseness." If I am wise and understanding of what God did for me in putting my sins on

Jesus and giving me His righteousness, then I am right-wise. When I permit Satan to tamper with this and take away my peace, I am "right-foolish." Sometimes when our works are not all they should be, we feel the least righteous; thus we lose our peace of mind and are robbed of our joy. When I receive Jesus, God's Son, I will fulfill and fully meet all of God's requirements. I will rejoice and laugh at the enemy when I understand my righteousness. I will not permit him to torment me over the past or needle me over my present lack of works. Understanding the cross of Christ brings joy. I will learn to laugh and have joy as I get understanding. Joy is a natural flow of the knowledge of salvation. This is why we can draw water out of the wells of salvation with joy. Isaiah 12:3. Righteousness and peace produce the joyful sound. It is a sound of "all is well with my soul."

The next time a remembrance of your old life bothers you, replace that thought with this one: "A brand new baby has no past." Begin to rejoice over this and also do not forget to extend this same right-wiseness to your brothers and sisters in Christ, who also began a new life without a past.

Notice the scriptures do not teach that we draw water out of the well of salvation with tears . . . even though the Bible has some good things to say about crying. A good verse for this is found in Psalm 30:5, "Weeping may endure for a night, but joy cometh in the morning." The Knox Translation puts it this way, "Sorrow is but the guest of a night, and joy comes in the morning." Dew says, "In the morning a song of joy." Certainly the Word doesn't teach us that we cry our way through life, but rather, we are supposed to laugh our way through. As a young pastor, I had a saint visit me who showed me how spiritual she was by carrying with her a shopping bag filled with soiled Kleenex tissues. She would have made a better impression had she just smiled. Most tears are a result of the feeling of loneliness . . .

or of being unloved and unappreciated. The feeling of being accepted in Christ, as we are, replaces with joy the tears of despondency.

All about us we view the ruins of many shipwrecked marriages. As a result of easy divorce, we are reaping many scarred lives. Many of them who were not in the church are now turning to the Lord and endeavoring to pick up the pieces. This is a crucial spiritual crisis time . . . one in which the children of God need to know their right-wiseness, or right-standing with God which erases the past, and to see themselves, clothed with white garments of righteousness before His throne. Their standing with God is based on Jesus' sacrifice, not on their own works, whether good or bad. The kingdom of God is not meat or drink, but righteousness, peace and joy in the Holy Ghost. This joy is a result of knowing the freedom that Christ gives from the sinful past and all its failures. This joy needs to be forcefully expressed — especially when Satan tries to hold your failures over your head. Joy flowing is laughing at the specter of the past . . . and enjoying our present position in Christ.

Dr. James Walsh said few persons realize that health actually varies according to the amount of laughter. Someone has said, "If laughter could be ordered at the corner drug store, doctors would prescribe many laughs a day." A sense of right-standing with God sets up a good environment for laughter.

Paul Rader has said, "When God chooses a man, He puts laughter into his life. God's Spirit moves into his heart and turns him right-side up. Old things pass away and become new. Now he has laughter in his soul."

In II Corinthians 10:4, we are taught to cast down imaginations and every high thing that exalteth itself against the knowledge of God. The one recurring thought that keeps cropping up in our imaginations is that we are not quite ready to stand before

God. We imagine ourselves as we see us, rather than how God sees us, for He sees us in white robes of righteousness, which is what we receive when we accept Christ. The next time you are worshipping God, picture yourself in that white robe of righteousness standing before the throne of God in perfect acceptance. See yourself made perfectly white by the blood of Jesus, God's Son. Don't let the enemy bring in sorrow or condemnation because of the past, but rather let the joy of laughter rise in your heart and flow out of your lips! Let Paul's admonition ring in your ears constantly, "Rejoice in the Lord always, again I say rejoice." Philippians 4:4.

A good illustration of using our imaginations in worship comes to us from a young pastor who related this story: "I saw myself in a long line waiting before the throne of the Lord Jesus. It seemed that each person moved along to await his turn before the Lord's throne. Some would kneel down, others would bow. I moved along to take my turn, but before I could bow or kneel, the Lord arose, stepped down from His throne, came to where I was standing, and took both of my hands in His and smiled. For the first time in my life I really felt that I was fully accepted by Him."

Being fully persuaded that God truly loves you and accepts you as you are makes it easy to picture yourself standing in His presence enjoying the pleasures that are at His right hand that now belong to you.

Time to Laugh:

A speaker, who had just received a rather grand introduction, took the podium and said, "I don't like to disagree with the fine statements just made about me, but, the fortune wasn't made in cotton, it was potatoes . . . and it wasn't $50,000 — it was $5,000 . . . and it wasn't me, it was my brother, and he didn't make it, he lost it."

Chapter XI

ROBBERS OF JOY

"At destruction and famine thou shalt laugh." Job 5:22a.

The Christian has not always been able to laugh at calamities. Most of the time these adverse situations rob us of the joy that we do have. Yet the scriptures teach that we can, that is, it is possible, to be able to have joy in all situations. What then robs us of our joy?

Hebrews 3:6 can help us:

"But Christ as a son over His own house; whose house are we, if we hold fast the confidence and the rejoicing of the hope firm unto the end."

The Greek word for confidence is, "parrhesia," to speak plainly, cheerfully — free from fear.

One can readily see why we are not prepared to laugh at destruction as Job 5:22a suggests. We fail to go around freely speaking cheerfully about our hope in Christ. We may speak of it if reminded, or in a gathering where others are discussing His coming. But to go around doing our daily task in joyful expressions is foreign in most Christian circles.

Our hope in Christ, our hope in His coming, or our hope in death if He doesn't return, is a hope that brings joy. Joy flowing is laughter, there is a glow of hope surrounding the child of God. Nothing but nothing can take this away if we hold it fast.

Romans 15:13:

"Now the God of hope fill you with all joy and peace in believing, that ye may abound in hope, through the power of the Holy Ghost."

In our believing, in our hope, we are filled with joy. That which robs us of our hope robs us of our joy and happiness. Destruction and famine cannot do injury to our hope, because our hope of His coming and eternal life isn't based on what happens. Therefore a child of God can stand in the midst of ruin, yes even sit in the ashes and laugh because nothing has happened to take away his hope — just material or physical possessions.

Full joy that no man can take, circumstances can't alter or deflate. It is the joy of our hope — Jesus is coming soon.

Perhaps all will be in agreement with me when I suggest that number one on everybody's list of joy robbers will be self-pity. There probably was never a person who didn't have to fight this. It is with us from childhood to old age. Self-pity is the result of being turned inward instead of being turned upward. The introvert fights that horrible feeling of failure on every hand, defeat in every task and embarrassment in every attempt. The next time you find yourself feeling sorry for yourself, look up to Jesus — see Him with your spiritual imagination smiling down upon you with love and nodding approval even if you fail. Self-pity was Israel's downfall. They wished they had died in Egypt or the wilderness. They did die in the wilderness because feeling sorry for themselves robbed them of faith, that robbed them of hope which in turn took their joy.

There will be many robbery attempts on your joy and hope in Jesus. Set yourself firm in His promises. See yourselves not in defeat, but in victory. Laugh now because we are all going to have a good one over there that shall last forever.

Time to Laugh:

A very discouraged layman went in to counsel with his pastor. He poured out his utter failure in all he tried to do. The pastor tried to encourage him by saying how easy it was to serve the Lord. The layman interupted him by saying, "Oh! Pastor I know you are successful and good, but you are paid to be good."

I guess the rest of us are just good for nothing!

He Who Laughs Lasts and Lasts and Lasts **is available at your local bookstore.**

HARRISON HOUSE
P. O. Box 35035
Tulsa, OK 74153

Roy H. Hicks is a successful minister of the Gospel who has given his life to pastoring and pioneering churches throughout the United States. He has served the Lord in various foreign fields, having made missionary journeys to South America, the Orient, Australia, and New Zealand.

As a dedicated man of God, Dr. Hicks formerly served as General Supervisor of the Foursquare Gospel Churches and has become a popular speaker at charismatic conferences.

Perhaps the things that most endear Dr. Hicks to readers is his warmth and his ability to reach out as the true believer he is—a man of strong, positive faith, sharing a refreshing ministry through the power and anointing of the Holy Spirit.

For a complete list of tapes and books
by Roy Hicks, write:

Dr. Roy H. Hicks,
P. O. Box 4113
San Marcos, California 92069

*Feel free to include your prayer requests and comments
when you write.*